The Little Book of
KITCHEN TABLE WISDOM

RACHEL NAOMI REMEN

edited by Jacqueline M. Berg

RIVERHEAD BOOKS
New York

THE BERKLEY PUBLISHING GROUP
Published by Penguin Group (USA) Inc.
375 Hudson Street, New York, New York 10014, USA

Penguin Group (Canada), 90 Eglinton Avenue East, Suite 700, Toronto, Ontario M4P 2Y3, Canada
(a division of Pearson Penguin Canada Inc.)
Penguin Books Ltd., 80 Strand, London WC2R 0RL, England
Penguin Group Ireland, 25 St. Stephen's Green, Dublin 2, Ireland (a division of Penguin Books Ltd.)
Penguin Group (Australia), 250 Camberwell Road, Camberwell, Victoria 3124, Australia
(a division of Pearson Australia Group Pty. Ltd.)
Penguin Books India Pvt. Ltd., 11 Community Centre, Panchsheel Park, New Delhi—110 017, India
Penguin Group (NZ), 67 Apollo Drive, Mairangi Bay, Auckland 1311, New Zealand
(a division of Pearson New Zealand Ltd.)
Penguin Books (South Africa)(Pty.) Ltd., 24 Sturdee Avenue, Rosebank, Johannesburg 2196, South Africa
Penguin Books Ltd., Registered Offices: 80 Strand, London WC2R 0RL, England

Portions of this book previously appeared in *Kitchen Table Wisdom, Stories That Heal*, by Rachel Naomi Remen, M.D., copyright © 1996 by Rachel Naomi Remen M.D. The names and identifying characteristics of the persons whose stories are told in this book have been changed to preserve their privacy.

First edition: April 2007

ISBN: 978-1-59448-250-2

This book has been registered with the Library of Congress.

PRINTED IN THE UNITED STATES OF AMERICA

10 9 8 7 6 5 4 3 2 1

In 1996 when *Kitchen Table Wisdom* was first published, I never dreamed this book of true stories would become important to so many people. It has now been translated into thirteen languages, and people all over the world have written to say it has eased their loneliness, reminded them of their worth, or helped them find strength and courage right at the center of their personal storm.

People have told me that they have read *Kitchen Table Wisdom* to each other in bed and kept it on their nightstands, or carried it on treks in the Himalayas, or taken it with them into surgery or radiation. They have given it to people who matter to them: their neighbors, their friends, their doctors, and their children. They have woven its stories into weddings and sermons and celebrations of all kinds. They have underlined and tabbed and cut out pages to carry in their pockets and purses. They have made it a part of their hearts and their lives.

To celebrate the tenth anniversary of *Kitchen Table Wisdom*, I have chosen a hundred or so thoughts (and a few of the shortest stories) from its pages, and made this little book for you. I sincerely hope it will be like an old friend—maybe a little worn down around the edges, maybe a coffee stain or two—but always there to remind you about what really matters in life.

—Rachel Naomi Remen, M.D.
Mill Valley, California
Spring 2006

CONTENTS

ABOUT STORIES

The real world is made of stories.

All stories matter. The wisdom in the story of the most educated and powerful person is often not greater than the wisdom in the story of a child, and the life of a child can teach us as much as the life of a sage.

When I was a child, people sat around kitchen tables and told their stories. We don't do that so much anymore. Sitting around the table telling stories is not just a way of passing time. It is the way the wisdom gets passed along. The stuff that helps us to live a life worth remembering. Despite the awesome powers of technology many of us still do not live very well. We may need to listen to each other's stories again.

Most parents know the importance of telling children their own story, over and over again, so that they come to know in the tellings who they are and to whom they belong. At the kitchen table we do this for each other. The stories at every kitchen table are about the same things, stories of owning, having and losing, stories of sex, of power, of pain, of wounding, of courage, hope and healing, of loneliness and the end of loneliness. In telling them, we are telling each other the human story. Stories that touch us in this place of connection awaken us and weave us together as a family once again.

Many of us do not know our own story. The story about who we are, not about what we have done. What we have faced to build what we have built, what we have drawn upon and risked to do it, what we have felt, thought, feared, and discovered through the events of our lives. What we have learned.

At the age of eighty-four my mother chose cardiac bypass surgery because it was the last chance she had for life. Even so, the odds were long: four chances in ten that she would not survive the operation. But my mother was not your ordinary elderly lady. She had lived her life as a maverick and a risk taker and to her those odds looked good. The morning of her surgery I came to her hospital room to kiss her before they took her upstairs. Despite the risk she was facing, my mother was peaceful.

"Oh good!" she greeted me. Pulling me close, she kissed me and whispered, "No matter what happens here, I want you to know that *I am satisfied*." Then she smiled her charming, rakish smile and they took her away. These were her final lucid words to me.

I thought about my mother's last words for a long time, trying to understand what she had meant. My mother had achieved a great deal in her life but I doubted that this had given her such ease and contentment in the face of almost certain death. She had left me with a question: How do I live so I, too, might find a deep satisfaction at the end of my life? The answer to this question still escapes me, but slowly I have come to understand that the question itself is an answer, a standard by which to measure every relationship, every decision, every risk. Like a story, a question is a fine traveling companion. It sharpens your eye for the road.

If we think we have no stories, we may not have paid enough attention to our lives. Most of us live far more meaningful lives than we know.

FINDING NEW EYES

Some years ago a young psychiatry resident who had come to learn more about people facing cancer was observing one of my patient sessions. A former gang member whose arms and hands were covered with tattoos was speaking of the deep love he now felt for his young wife who was dying of cancer; the ways in which his capacity to love had caught him unawares and so had healed him. In the language of the streets he shared profound insights about himself and his suffering and experiences of intense intimacy and tenderness with his wife. I glanced over at the young Freudian psychiatrist. He had stopped taking his usual feverish notes. His eyes were filled with tears. After this patient left, I asked him if he had learned anything useful from the session. He smiled ruefully. "We are all more than we seem," he said.

A label is a mask that life wears.

The relationships in which we are truly seen and heard are holy relationships. They remind us of our value as human beings. They give us the strength to go on. Eventually they may even help us to transform our pain into wisdom.

What we believe about ourselves can hold us hostage.

Every victim may be a survivor who does not know it yet.

We may need to take our experts far more lightly. Some years ago I served on the PhD committee of a woman in Moscow, Idaho, who was studying spontaneous healing of cancer. Looking for research subjects, she placed an ad in the local paper asking people who thought they healed from cancer in ways that defied explanation to contact her and tell her their story. Among the people who answered was a farmer who had done exceptionally well despite a dire cancer prognosis. On the phone one evening, she told me about him. She felt his amazing outcome was related to his attitude. "He didn't take it on," she said.

Confused, I asked her if he had denied that he had cancer. No, she said. He had just taken the same attitude toward his physician's prognosis that he took toward the words of the government soil experts who analyzed his fields. As they were educated men, he respected them and listened carefully as they showed him the findings of their tests and told him that the corn would not grow in this field. He valued their opinions. But, as he told my student, "A lot of the time the corn grows anyway."

Sometimes all that is needed is a sense of possibility.

Not long ago I was walking in the rain in the place where I was born, New York City, thinking of the green place where I now live, grateful for the ease with which things grow there. Not all things grow easy. The rain made me intensely aware of the hardness and grayness of this world of cement and brick. For miles and miles there seemed to be nothing living that could respond to the rain. But the rain comes anyway. The possibility of growth is there even in the hardest times.

There is a wisdom in remaining open to the possibility of growth in any circumstances without ever knowing what shape that growth may take.

BECOMING WHOLE

The first house I owned was a little A-frame cabin near the top of a mountain outside of San Francisco. When I bought it, it was so cramped and shabby that the first friend who saw it blurted out, "Oh, Rachel, you bought *this*?" The day after I moved in I started throwing things away, and for the next few years I threw away all sorts of things: light fixtures, toilets, staircases, doors. Eventually, I even took out some ceilings and walls.

Oddly, the more I threw away, the more I seemed to have. As I let go of each thing, I could imagine my father saying, "Just a minute, that still works, you never know when you'll need one of those." Gradually, the house became simpler, emptier, and the beautiful structural lines of its basic form began to emerge. Eventually it became whole and filled with light.

Wholeness lies beyond perfection.

As a child, when I brought home a ninety-eight on an exam, my father always asked, "What happened to the other two points?" My childhood became focused on the pursuit of those two points. It took years to discover that those points don't really matter. That they don't make you lovable. Or whole. That they are not the secret of living a life worth remembering.

Perfectionism is the belief that life is broken.

We are capable of fear and courage, generosity and selfishness, vulnerability and strength. These things do not cancel each other out but offer us a full range of power and response to life.

Over time, our vulnerability may become our strength, our fear may develop our courage, and our woundedness may be the road to our integrity.

TEACHERS AND HEALERS

Often it is our imperfections and even our pain that draws others close to us. Just as often, our own experience of pain enables others who hurt to be open with us without feeling small. Our wounds make us trustworthy.

In the presence of certain people we may get to try on a greater wholeness for a time, to actually experience being more. These experiences are a sort of grace. They help us to know not only the direction of our personal wholeness but also how it feels and even tastes.

We are all healers.

We all influence one another. We are a part of each other's reality. Perhaps there is no such thing as passing someone and not having a moment of connection.

There is enormous power in the simplest of human relation-ships: the strength of a touch, the blessing of forgiveness, the grace of someone else taking you just as you are and finding in you an unsuspected goodness.

The year he went bankrupt, my father bought me a pair of elegant real gold earrings. Opening the box they came in, I had stared at them in a thirteen-year-old's silence, bewildered, feeling the weight of my homeliness, my shyness, my hopeless difference from my classmates who easily joked and flirted and laughed. "Aren't you going to try them on?" asked my father, so I took them to my room and put them on my ears. Cautiously I looked in the mirror. My pimply face and lank hair looked much as always. The earrings looked absurd.

Tearing them from my ears I rushed back into the living room and flung them on the floor. "How could you do this?" I shrieked at my father. "I'm too ugly to wear them. How could you waste all that money?" Then I burst into tears. My father said nothing until I had cried myself out. Then he passed me his clean, folded handkerchief. "I know they don't suit you right

38

now," he said quietly. "I bought them because someday they will suit you perfectly."

My adolescence was a time of profound self-doubt. At some of the darkest moments, I would get out the earrings and look at them. My father had spent a hundred dollars he did not have because he saw the person I would become in time. He believed in that person, and this made all the difference.

When it comes to healing others, our life experience is as valuable as any credential.

Most people have come to prefer certain of life's experiences and deny and reject others, unaware of the value of the things that come wrapped in plain or even ugly paper. In avoiding all pain and seeking comfort at all cost, we may be left without intimacy or compassion; in rejecting change and risk, we often cheat ourselves of discovery; in denying our suffering, we may never know our strength or greatness.

There are times when our ability to teach and heal becomes stronger. Dying people often have the power to heal the rest of us in powerful ways. Years afterwards, many people can remember what a dying person has said to them and carry it with them, woven into the fabric of their being, enabling them to live better.

Some people heal because they have work to do. Others heal because they have been released from their work and the pressures and expectations placed on them. Some people need music, others need silence; some need people around them, others heal alone. The ways in which we heal are as unique as our fingerprints.

There is no statute of limitations on healing.

Things that can never be fixed can still heal.

We carry the potential of healing with us even into the darkest of our inner places.

Our life force may not require us to strengthen it. We often just need to free it where it has gotten trapped by beliefs, attitudes, judgment, and shame.

When we look deeply and honestly at our own wounds, we discover our power, experience our will to live, our courage, and our ability to heal ourselves over and over again.

LOSS

Often in times of loss as we reach for what we have considered to be our strength, we may stumble on our wholeness and our real power.

Nothing ever ends without something else beginning or begins without something else ending.

Grieving is what enables you to go forward after a loss. It heals you so that you can love again.

If we fear loss enough, in the end the things we possess will come to possess us.

More than anything else, the way we deal with loss shapes our capacity to be fully alive. The way we protect ourselves from loss may be the way in which we distance ourselves from life.

For many years I tried to persuade my elderly father to buy a new living room couch. Year after year, the old green couch grew shabbier and shabbier. Finally it was no longer safe to sit on. Embarrassed, I told Dad that I had called and ordered a new couch from Macy's and was sending a photograph of it. If he liked it, they would deliver it on Friday. He loved it.

On Saturday I called. How did it look? Shamefacedly, my father told me he had canceled the delivery. It turned out that he didn't know what to do with the old couch. I suggested calling Macy's and telling them to take it away. He told me that they did not do that there in New York.

"Then how about the Salvation Army?" But apparently they only took away the things they could still sell. Who would want his couch? With a sinking heart, I suggested looking in the

Yellow Pages for someone who does hauling. But Dad was afraid to have a stranger come to his home.

Finally I was silenced. My father, unaccustomed to letting go of anything, could not find a way to accept my gift. Several years later, in the night, the old couch collapsed in on itself. It stood that way until my father died and I brought my mother to live with me in California.

Times of loss are times of discovery, periods when we cannot maintain our old ways of doing things and enter into a steep learning curve. Sometimes it takes loss to initiate growth.

Jane's gentle brown dog was never more than a few feet from her. Its love and devotion were returned full measure, and when it died of old age, my friend said that she doubted she could ever have another dog.

Over the next few years, I visited her often in the small beach town where she lived. Sunday afternoons we would walk down to the beach together. In those few blocks, she would stop to pat dogs on leashes, and strays would come up joyfully to greet her. Each got a moment of tenderness and a dog biscuit from her pocket.

Once I asked her if she still missed her dog. "Yes," she said, "very much." But then she went on to say that over time things had changed for her. When she had a dog, there were only two kinds of dogs: her dog and all other dogs. When he died, she was brokenhearted. But now it seems to her as if all dogs somehow belong to her and fill the empty place in her heart.

Anything good you've ever been given is yours forever.

SUFFERING

Becoming numb to suffering will not make us happy.

Suffering is intimately connected to wholeness.

The part in us that feels suffering is the same as the part that feels joy.

My patient, a physician who has cancer, comes to his session and tells me this story:

Shiva and Shakti, the Divine Couple in Hinduism, are in their heavenly abode watching over the earth. They are touched by the challenges of human life and the ever-present place of suffering in the human experience. One day, Shakti spies a miserably poor man walking down a road. His clothes are shabby and his sandals are tied together with rope. Her heart is wrung with compassion. Touched by his goodness and his struggle, Shakti turns to her divine husband and begs him to give this man some gold. Shiva looks at the man for a long moment. "My Dearest Wife," he says, "I cannot do that."

Shakti is astounded. "Why, what do you mean, Husband? You are Lord of the Universe. Why can't you do this simple thing?"

"I cannot give this to him because he is not yet ready to receive it," Shiva replies.

66

Shakti becomes angry, "Do you mean to say that you cannot drop a bag of gold in his path?"

"Surely I can," Shiva replies, "but that is quite another thing."

"Please, Husband," says Shakti. And so Shiva drops a bag of gold in the man's path.

Meanwhile the man walks along thinking to himself, "I wonder if I will find dinner tonight—or shall I go hungry again?" Turning a bend in the road, he sees something on the path in his way. "Aha," he says. "Look there, a big rock! How fortunate that I have seen it! I might have tripped and torn these poor sandals of mine even further." Carefully stepping over the bag of gold, he goes on his way, congratulating himself on his good fortune.

The bags of gold that life drops in our path rarely look like what they are at first. I ask my patient if he has ever recognized a bag of gold on his path and used it to enrich his life. He smiles at me. "Cancer," he says simply.

Personal peace is not achieved by armoring yourself against the suffering around you or within you. Inner peace is more a question of cultivating perspective and meaning even as life touches you with its pain: more a question of wisdom than a position of distance.

Suffering shapes the life force, sometimes into anger, sometimes into blame and self-pity. Eventually it may show us the wisdom of embracing and loving life.

Perhaps the healing of the world rests on a shift in our way of seeing, a coming to know that in our suffering and our joy we are connected to one another with unbreakable and compelling human bonds.

ALIVENESS

Life is not a possession.

From people with cancer I have learned how to enjoy the minute particulars in life once again, the grace of a hot cup of coffee, the presence of a friend, the blessing of having a new cake of soap or an hour without pain.

The fewer preferences we have about life, the more deeply we can experience and participate in life. Aliveness is more about discovery than about having your own way.

It is possible to have a good life even though it is not an easy life.

Joy is far less fragile than happiness. Joy seems to come from an unconditional wish to live, the willingness to accept life whole and show up to make the most of whatever is there. It has a kind of invincibility that attachment to any particular outcome would deny us.

Fulfilling our life's purpose may depend more on how we play than what we are dealt.

What we do to survive is often different from what we may need to do in order to live.

There is a tenacity toward life present in every cell without which even the most sophisticated of medical interventions would not succeed.

Coherent, elegant, mysterious, aesthetic. When I first earned my degree in medicine, I would not have described life in this way. But I was not on intimate terms with life then. I had not seen the power of the life force in everyone, met the will to live in all its varied, subtle forms, recognized the irrepressible love of life buried in the heart of every living thing. I had not been used by life to fulfill itself or been caught unaware by its strength in the midst of the most profound weakness. I had no sense of awe. I had thought that life was broken and that I, armed with the powerful tools of modern science, could fix it. But life has shown me otherwise.

There is a difference between impermanence and fragility. Life can change abruptly and end without warning, but life is not fragile.

Given the nature of life, there may be no security, but only adventure.

Embracing life is a choice.

CHOOSING LIFE

Sometimes we may need to simply choose life. It is possible to become so attached to something or someone we have lost that we move forward blindly, looking over our shoulder to the past rather than before us to what lies ahead. The Bible tells us that as she looked back, Lot's wife was turned into a pillar of salt. I suspect that many of us have had this happen to us without our realizing. We have become frozen, trapped by the past. We are holding on to something long gone and, hands full, are unable to take hold of our opportunities or what life is offering.

When asked to describe her husband, my patient laughs and tells this story about a trip to Hawaii. An organized and frugal man, her husband had reserved compact rental cars on each of the four islands months in advance. Arriving on the Big Island, they presented their reservation to the car rental desk and were told that the economy car they had reserved was not available. Alarmed, she had watched her husband's face redden as he prepared to do battle. The clerk did not seem to notice. "I am so sorry, sir," he said. "Will you accept a substitute for the same price? We have a Mustang convertible." Barely mollified, her husband put their bags in this beautiful white sports car and they drove off.

The same thing happened throughout their holiday. They would turn in their car and fly to the next island, only to be told that the car they had been promised was not available and offered a same price substitution. It was amazing, she said. After the Mustang, they had been given a Mazda MR-10, a Lincoln Town Car, and finally, a Mercedes, all with the most sincere apologies. The vacation was wonderful and on the plane back she turned to her husband, thanking him for all he had done to arrange such a memorable time. "Yes," he said, pleased, "it was really nice. But too bad they never had the right car for us." He was not joking.

Sometimes we become married to our expectations and miss a love affair with life.

Our beliefs change the way we actually experience our lives. A belief is like a pair of sunglasses. When we wear a belief and look at life through it, it is difficult to convince ourselves that what we see is not green.

Life usually offers us far more than our biases and preferences will allow us to have.

We may need to let go of our beliefs and ideas about life in order to have life.

When necessary, we can choose the inevitable.

A certain percentage of those who have survived near-death experiences report catching a glimpse of life's basic lesson plan. We are all here for a single purpose: to grow in wisdom and to learn to love better. We can do this through losing as well as through winning, by having and by not having, by succeeding or by failing. All we need to do is to show up openhearted for class.

LOVE

The opening of the heart seems to go far beyond love to an experience of belonging that heals our deepest wounds.

All love is unconditional. Anything else is just approval.

Approval is a form of judgment. When we approve of people, we sit in judgment on them as surely as when we criticize them.

The life in us is diminished by judgment far more frequently than by disease.

One moment of unconditional love may call into question a lifetime of feeling unworthy and invalidate it.

As a child I spent many summers alone on a deserted beach on Long Island, gathering shells, digging for little clams, leading a far different life from the city life I led the rest of the year. There was great peace in these summers, a new ability to be without people and yet not alone, and I have many good memories of this time. Every morning the sea would wash up new treasures— pieces of wood from sunken boats, bits of glass worn smooth as silk, the occasional jellyfish. Some of my most vivid memories concerned the beautiful white birds that flew constantly over- head. I remember how their wings would become transparent when they passed between me and the sun. Angel wings. My heart followed them and yearned for wings to fly.

Many years later I had the opportunity to walk this same beach. It was a great disappointment. Bits of seaweed and gar- bage littered the shoreline, and there were sea gulls everywhere, screaming raucously, fighting over the garbage and the occasional dead creature the sea had given up.

Disheartened, I drove home. It was only later that I realized that the gulls were the white birds of my childhood. The beach had not changed. In the absence of judgment, many things can become holy.

Few of us are able to love ourselves as we are.

Each of us is unfinished. If life is process, all judgments are provisional. We can't judge anything until it is complete. No one has won or lost until the race is over.

One of the blessings of growing older is the discovery that many of the things I once believed to be my shortcomings have turned out in the long run to be my strengths, and other things of which I was unduly proud have revealed themselves in the end to be among my shortcomings. What a blessing it is to outlive your self-judgments and harvest your failures.

CONNECTION

Communication is not always connection.

The most valuable thing we ever give each other is our attention. And especially when we give it from the heart.

We connect through listening. A loving silence often has far more power to heal and to connect than the most well intentioned words.

I have long suspected that a sense of isolation and aloneness may undermine the will to live. For more than twenty years I have used a simple way to help people facing radiation, chemotherapy, or surgery to remember that they are not alone. I suggest they find an ordinary stone, small enough to fit into their hand, and invite their closest friends and family to a meeting. It does not matter how large or small the meeting is, but it is important that it be made up of those who are connected to them through a bond of the heart.

The process is simple and intimate. People sit in a circle in silence and the stone is passed from hand to hand. One by one, each person holds it and tells the story of a time when they too faced a crisis. People may talk about the loss of jobs or dreams or relationships, or about illness or death. When they finish telling their story, they take a moment to reflect on a personal quality that they feel helped them through that difficult time and name it out loud. People will say such things as, "What brought me through was stubbornness," "What brought me through was faith," or "What brought me through was a sense of humor." When they have named their strength, they speak directly to the one who invited them to the meeting, saying, "I put stubbornness into this stone for you," or "I put faith into this stone for you."

Often what people say is surprising. Sometimes they tell stories that happened when they were young or in wartime and share things that others, even family members, may not have known before, or they attribute their survival to qualities that are not ordinarily seen as strengths.

Many of my patients bring their stone with them to chemotherapy or radiation and some have even gone into surgery with their stone strapped to the palm of their hand or the bottom of their foot with adhesive tape.

No one has chemotherapy or radiation or goes into an operating room without the thoughts, hopes, and prayers of others going with them. The stone makes all of that visible, tangible, real.

Listening creates a holy silence. When you listen generously to people, they can hear the truth in themselves, often for the first time. And when you listen deeply, you can know yourself in everyone.

REFUGE

The way to freedom from fear often lies through an open heart.

A woman came in after missing an appointment and told me that she had been in the emergency room last week at the time she was supposed to be here in my office. I had not known this and I asked her what had happened. She told me that she had suffered a temporary blockage of her intestine. The pain had been severe and lasted for a day, but now it was over. When the pain began, she had recognized it as something of significance. She had packed a small bag, putting in her makeup, a nightie, and a mystery she was in the middle of reading. Then she had driven herself twenty-five miles to the hospital.

Having experienced intestinal obstructions myself, I knew how severe such pain could be. I asked her how she had managed. She told me that she had driven until the pain came, then she had pulled off the road and waited for it to pass. She had been very sick but she had gotten to the hospital. It had taken a long time. Surprised, I asked her why she had not called a friend. She told me it was the middle of the day and everyone was working.

She had spent the next day in the emergency room alone. I asked her why she hadn't called anyone even then. "Why would I call anyone?" she responded with irritation. "None of my friends know a thing about intestinal obstruction."

"Jessie," I said, "even children instinctively run to others when they hurt." With a great deal of heat she replied, "I've never understood that. It's so silly. Kissing the boo-boo doesn't help the pain at all." I was stunned. "Jessie," I said, "it doesn't help the pain, it helps the loneliness."

Many people think they need to be alone with their pain. When Jessie was in pain, the only thing she sought from others was their expertise. Her mother had died when she was born. It had never occurred to her that anything could be done about the loneliness.

As I age, I am grateful to find that a silence has begun to gather in me, coexisting with my tempers and my fears, unchanged by my joys or my pain. A place of refuge, connected to the Silence everywhere.

In a book about Spain, I remember reading that there is a place in the bullring, different for every bull, where the bull feels safe. If he can reach this place he stops running and can gather his full strength. In the presence of the matador, he is no longer afraid.

In bullfighting, this place of refuge is called the *querencia*. For people, the *querencia* is a place in our inner world. Sometimes it is a viewpoint, a position from which to conduct a life, different for each person.

Often it is simply a place of deep inner peace.

Healing is possible even in the absence of cure. Cure is about the recovery of the body. Healing is about the recovery of the soul.

HOLINESS

When you come right down to it, life is holy.

Because our true value is anchored in the sacred, it is unchanging, impervious to disease or age. It lies beyond our usefulness, our possessions, our skills, or our personal power. Most of us have an innate sense of the sacredness of every human life. An expert lost is replaceable; a human being lost is not.

God's presence is an experience that never changes. It's a relationship that's there all the time, even when we're not paying attention to it. Perhaps the Infinite holds us to Itself in the same way the earth does. Like gravity, if it ever stopped we would know it instantly. But it never does.

Years ago Joseph Campbell offered a workshop for a group of physicians on the experience of the sacred. At one point he showed us slide after slide of sacred images: paintings, statues, pottery, and stained glass from many places and times. I remember one of these vividly. It was a particularly fine example of Shiva Nataraja, a "Dancing Shiva." Shiva is the Hindu name for the supreme God and while these small statues are now rather common, few of us had seen this charming image before.

The specific statue portrayed Shiva dancing in a ring of bronze flames. The hands of his many arms hold symbols of the abundance of spiritual life. One of his feet is lifted high and the other is resting on the back of a little man crouched down in the dirt, holding a leaf between his hands and studying it with great intensity.

We were all intrigued by this little man, and we asked Joseph Campbell about him and why he was focused so intently on the leaf between his hands. Campbell began to laugh. Still laughing, he told us that perhaps the little man is a person so caught up in the reality of the material world that he doesn't know that the living God is dancing on his back. There is a bit of that little man in us all.

Perhaps the wisdom lies not in the constant struggle to bring the sacred into our daily life but in the recognition that there may be no daily life, that life is committed and whole and despite appearances, we are always on sacred ground.

Life itself may be a spiritual practice.

Prayer is not a way to get what we want.

Prayer may be less about asking for the things we are attached to than it is about relinquishing our attachments.

It can take us beyond fear, which is an attachment, and beyond hope, which is another form of attachment.

It can help us remember the nature of the world and the nature of life, not on an intellectual level but in a deep and experiential way.

When we pray, we don't change the world, we change ourselves.

We change our consciousness.

We move from an individual, isolated making-things-happen kind of consciousness to connection on the deepest level with the largest possible reality.

Turning towards prayer is a release from the arrogance and vulnerability of individual causality.

When we pray, we stop trying to control life and remember that we belong to life.

It is an opportunity to experience humility and grace.

Prayer is a movement from mastery to mystery.

As a human being, I can never hope to have the depth and breadth of perspective to know whether any of my actions will ultimately harm or heal.

Yet I hope that I may be used to serve a holy purpose without ever knowing.

Perhaps there is only one prayer: "In this moment, I am here. Use me."

Ritual helps us experience something which is already real. It does not create the sacred; it only makes visible what is there and has always been there, deeply hidden in the obvious.

Much of life can never be explained but only witnessed.

Perhaps life can be trusted.